AF411563

Ghost Wrestling

Also by Roger Weingarten

POETRY

Infant Bonds of Joy
Shadow, Shadow
Ethan Benjamin Boldt
Tables of the Meridian
The Love and Death Boy
The Vermont Suicides
What Are Birds Worth

ANTHOLOGIES

New American Poets of the '90s (with Jack Myers)
New American Poets of the '80s (with Jack Myers)
Love Stories, Love Poems (with Joe David Bellamy)

Ghost Wrestling

Poems by

Roger Weingarten

DAVID R. GODINE, *Publisher*
Boston

First published in 1997 by
DAVID R. GODINE, Publisher
Box 9103
Lincoln, Massachusetts 01773

Library of Congress Cataloging-in-Publication Data

Weingarten, Roger.
Ghost wrestling : poems / by Roger Weingarten.
   p.   cm.
ISBN 1-56792-039-X
   I. Title.
PS3573.E3957G46   1995
   811'.54—DC20
   95-17834
   CIP

First edition
This book was printed on acid-free paper
Printed and bound in the United States of America

For Eli, Jonah, and Sarah

Acknowledgments

Acknowledgment is gratefully made to the following periodicals in which versions of these poems first appeared:

The American Poetry Review: "In the Cloud Chamber";
The Bloomsbury Review: "Coming into Rabat," "Passover in the French Quarter";
Crazyhorse: "Objects in Mirror Are Closer Than They Appear";
Green Mountains Review: "The Life and Times of My Last Idea," "Parable of the First Frost";
The Louisville Review: "The Latin Jazz," "Passover Mud";
Michigan Quarterly Review: "The Spectral Illumination of Moonshine";
Mississippi Review: "Rapid Transit, July 1955";
The Missouri Review: "Dear Mike," "Jungle Gliders," "Stomping the Beaver Palace";
The Nebraska Review: "Meditation on a Swollen Bladderwort," "Portrait of the Artist Relieving Himself in Le Bois Sacré";
The North American Review: "Crawling Between Earth and Heaven";
The Paris Review: "E.S.P.," "Geography IV," "P.S.";
Passages North: "Villanelle of the Crucified and the Risen Christ";
Ploughshares: "Ornamental Agony of December";
Poetry: "The Afterlife";
Poetry East: "Against Friendship," "The New Confessions";
Poetry Miscellany: "Night on Bear Mountain," "The Dark Gold Hummock of Desire";
The Prague Review: "Objects in Mirror Are Closer Than They Appear," "Aura, Cry, Fall and Fit," "In the Cloud Chamber," "Jungle Gliders";
Shenandoah: "Aura, Cry, Fall and Fit," "Moment of Vaulted Chambers";
Western Humanities Review: "Amber," "Ghost Wrestling."

"The Latin Jazz" won the 1994 Louisville Review Poetry Prize.

"Stomping the Beaver Palace" was reprinted in *Anthology of World Farm Poems* (University of Iowa Press, 1997).

"Moment of Vaulted Chambers" was reprinted in *The San Diego Reader* (1996).

"In the Cloud Chamber" was reprinted in *Family: A Celebration* (Peterson's, 1995) and in *Pushcart Prize XVIII: Best of the Small Presses* (Pushcart Press, 1993).

"Villanelle of the Crucified and the Risen Christ" was reprinted in *Passages North Anthology* (Milkweed Editions, 1990).

Heartfelt thanks to Alice Fulton, Richard Jackson, Ellen Lesser, and Mark Polizzotti for their generous readership and suggestions, and to the Dana Foundation and The Vermont Council on the Arts for awards that helped me complete this collection.

Contents

JUNGLE GLIDERS
Stomping the Beaver Palace / 3
The Latin Jazz / 5
Objects In Mirror Are Closer Than They Appear / 7
Coming Into Rabat / 10
Geography IV / 12
E.S.P. / 13
Meditation on a Swollen Bladderwort / 15
P.S. / 17
Crawling Between Earth and Heaven / 19
Jungle Gliders / 22

THE FIVE SEASONS
The Life and Times of My Last Idea / 27
Ornamental Agony of December / 29
Passover Mud / 31
Night on Bear Mountain / 32
Parable of the First Frost / 35

THE SPECTRAL ILLUMINATION OF MOONSHINE
The Afterlife / 39
Portrait of the Artist Relieving Himself in Le Bois Sacré / 41
Aura, Cry, Fall and Fit / 43
Passover in the French Quarter / 48
Villanelle of the Crucified and the Risen Christ / 50
The Dark Gold Hummock of Desire / 51
The Ayatollah of I Told You So / 53
The Spectral Illumination of Moonshine / 55

GHOST WRESTLING

In the Cloud Chamber   /   61

Amber   /   63

Dear Mike   /   65

Moment of Vaulted Chambers   /   70

The New Confessions   /   74

Rapid Transit, July 1955   /   77

Against Friendship   /   79

Ghost Wrestling   /   82

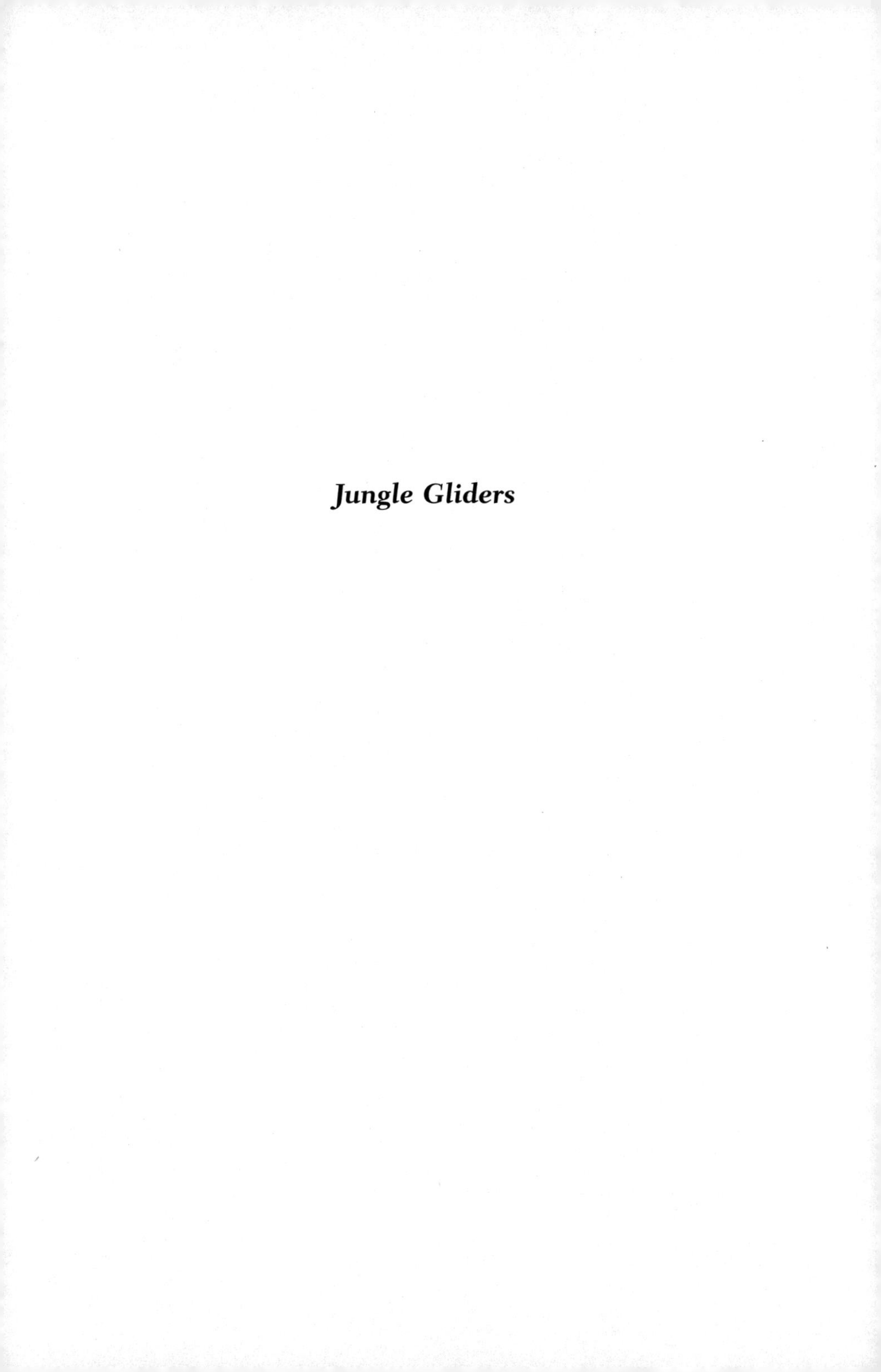

Jungle Gliders

Stomping the Beaver Palace

Water flows down the mountain
into a clawfoot tub in the cellar,
where I circle a skunk curled up
in the furnace and a half-blind
vole feasting on a plate
of poisoned wheat. Sometimes
the water pipe jutting
out of fieldstone seizes
up in winter, sometimes the World
War II water heater pilot
blows itself out, or I get the urge
to watch the groundthaw in April
purl into a sump pump
buried in the coal-studded floor,
scrape my skull against a square-head nail
pounded into a beam a century
and a half ago by the farmer who hollowed
out a future in unobliging soil
and aim my flashlight into the crawlspace,
where a predator made a furious meal
of a mourning dove. I crawl in
and twig to how it feels to orbit
a planet in a tin can. From this eye socket
perch, I press my palm to the light
like a fortuneteller revealing the red-
shadowed future of my bones, turn it off
to see myself in the dark execute
a buck and wing on the mud-and-stick
tiled roof of a beaver palace, then slap
and dive toward the entrance
into the catacomb. Upstairs, and still

bristling at my refusal to attend
courses in synchronized
breathing and belly-dancing, my wife
spears the blackened remnants
out of the toaster, our child,
upside-down and floating
inside her, ready to scream.

The Latin Jazz

She dragged a brush through red
highlights and stared at his

reflection over her shoulder,
sweeping lint from her collar

with the back of his hand.
As the pale lipstick snaked

across her lip, like the ghost
of someone else's finger,

he was certain the male half
of the couple they were expecting

was the reason she turned
away from his body turning toward her,

awake or asleep. She slid
the toothpick into the bread. He pulled

the cork from the bottle. She hung
up the phone and said, They can't

make it: his wife's morning sickness,
the ride. A candlelit

dinner for two's slow procession
from glasses clicking

to us, they both said, to the bird
stuffed with questions that dissolved

into accusations met with silence. He
punched the wall. She dabbed

antiseptic on broken skin. They made love
like an unwinnable argument. He left

for work, returning in the early
afternoon to find

them on the rug bent over
liner notes for the Latin jazz

he'd never heard before. He stepped
over them, raked the needle across the record,

then walked out to stab the button
between the elevator and mirror, where he saw

a man crying or
laughing at himself, he wasn't sure.

He closed his fist around a subway
token in his pocket, and waited

for the stranger to grow familiar.

Objects In Mirror Are Closer Than They Appear

The hour glass on the black
widow's back hovers in a shrub.

I watch the one-legged
nude walk upstairs and reach

through a window toward a helicopter
searchlight scanning a body

draped over a dumpster as a glass elevator,
like a paperweight filled

with luminous miniatures, climbs
up and down the hotel in the background.

The last grapefruit falls from a branch
into the irrigation ditch alive with henna-

colored roaches mounting each other. Dust
devils intertwine in a vacant lot.

A woman in a trance, running her fingers
through Egyptian sands, exorcises

primitive ghosts from her carport.
Oleander roots break into sewer pipe

while the night collapses. The air
inverts. I smile at the pillow

where only yesterday I relieved my wife of all
responsibility, then putted my way

through Miniature Golf-O-Rama; wore mirrored
shades into the swamp-cooled used furniture

warehouse of mildewed wrap-around sofas,
peeling credenzas, and a closed-circuit

camera stuck in a cactus; followed a ramp
into the underground garage, then took

the sit-down escalator into the hi-rise
nursing home of my ancestors in time

for visiting hours; ate three
rellenos, a steak and pie; sold my car

for more than I paid for it. Tonight,
silhouettes of palms will press

the turquoise sunset, an occasional
tarantula will twitch and graze. High above

this allergy-free, ever-expanding
metropolis, I'll lean back against the first

governor's pyramid glowing in the dark, ream
the bore of my rifle clean, fix

the telescope to its mount, slip
the cartridge clip into the magazine, and wait

for the daybreak commuter traffic.
This is the press kit for your visit, a souvenir

hourglass turned upside-down. These
are the answers to your questions, the mirror

you can use to look in the mirror
at yourself looking into the mirror.

This is the life.

Coming into Rabat

Out of the crush
of hooded men and blue
tears tattooed
down the cheeks of women

muttering to milky-eyed
infants and crates of chickens,
a hand out of nowhere on my wrist:
a hash dealer who hustled me

around an aromatic pyramid
of flowers and fruit, a woman
gathering raw silk into skeins
on her fingers, and livers

skewered and sweating in the sun,
before I begged
him to get lost, then hurried
to my bus through a cloud of children

that opened to reveal the cat-sized
gray rat they were torturing
that looked a little like
the hash dealer following

in my wake to the seat behind the driver's,
where he spat in my face. Jew,
he hissed to the double
row of strangers, who nodded. He makes more
in a week than I do in fifty, and he still
won't buy my good shit.

They nodded again. He let
his hand drop to the hem of his gray-striped

djellaba, the handle visible
above the crisscrossed
straps around the hairless ankle,
but the driver turned

and grabbed his wrist. We pulled away
from Tangier, from his fingers shaking
the foil-wrapped hash, then I rode my headache
into sleep. When the driver shook me

and pointed to the open door, I stepped
off into the sunset reflected
in a puddle of oil-
slicked urine.

Geography IV

Until he followed her into the stairwell
of the parking garage, he was no one.

Until he tried to bend her backward
over the metal bannister, holding a blade

to the side of her throat, he was camoflauged
against the gray concrete. Until she grabbed

his belt buckle and with the other hand
dropped the bloodshot

eye of her cigarette into his almost
extinct volcano, even his Eagle

Scout son got lost trying
to find his hideout. She kicked him

unconscious, severed his ring
finger with his folding hunter,

then held it like a torch
for the automatic

cameras of the press swarming
like yellow jackets over the contour

map of marriage in the New World, August,
1990.

E.S.P.

I was watching the last minutes
of the '76 Summer Olympics when

guess whose fingers covered my eyes,
her wet suit pressed between

her raised nipple and my shoulder blade?
I imagined a Red Sea

of eyes around the globe
glued to the hundred French

Canadian Catholic school girls
dancing into the five

Olympic circles. Through her fingers
parted like Venetian blinds, I spied

the twirling crush of long skirts,
the flares of flash attachments,

and glowsticks, like sea urchins,
flickering in the engorged

stadium. Eyes
in the back of my head, an endangered

species, scanned the tip
of her tongue between her lips. There was

a hush and groan
in Montreal and in our furnished

room in the Bible belt, just
as the voiceover assured us that

what we were witnessing—the gendarme
running with towel after the pale

scalloped cheeks of the streaker, who
cut a path bearing his own Olympic

torch into the interlocking
circles that scattered

across the great screen above the stadium
of the international dream—was not
on the program.

Meditation on a Swollen Bladderwort

While the periodontist removed stitches
with a surgical tweezers, a psychologist

on her radio said, It's time that men
became more monogamous. I remembered

sitting on the steps with my wife's
professor, a father four times over, married

to a woman with cancer, pouring a blender
of something thick and yellow into his glass.

While he was going on about Conrad's
"Secret Sharer," invisible pheasants

squawked in the cornfield, and we rushed
into the tall thicket to try and flush one.

Tightly wound on what he thought
was the middle of his life, he left his wife

for happier days with mine, but died,
after proving that criticism was superior

to poetry, a few years later of a heart attack.
What about married women? I asked, spitting

into the miniature whirlpool. Are they
so goddamned innocent? Laughing

through her sterile mask, she said,
Sit back so I can dress your gum, and relax

or I'll sew you up again. While she pressed
the putty into the nooks and crannies, a wildflower

expert described a yellow-flowered
carnivore levitated

over water above a wheel
of bloated stalks and egg-shaped

bladders equipped
with trigger-hairs on mouths that swell to suck

the prey inside the plant, which struck me
as the perfect portrait of my old rival

and his need. Then I remembered
high cheek bones and stray

blond hairs over the half-closed eyes
of my student

I was seeing at the time. I touched
the doctor on her wrist, who removed

her finger from my mouth, looking at me
like she was waiting for a question.

P.S.

Don't forget that while my legs
were clamped around the mule's
ribs climbing a defunct

streambed into the cloud forest
of Costa Rica, I was picturing your lips
pursed as you cut your diaphragm

into confetti, and I, like a sperm
genetically programmed
to swim in reverse, backed

out of our future into Central America
to catch my breath. The mule
didn't press me, but when the trail

turned steep, it sent my renegade
carcass into a nosedive that ended
in a tree overhanging a cliff.

Like a Hyacinth Macaw
screaming across the gorge,
your laughter smashed against the bars

of my concussion. Brooklyn Bob,
the guide, paid no mind when I declared
I was hunky-dory. He lifted me like an armload

of saplings to the beast and whipped us
all the way to the cloud forest
infirmary, where my leg is elevated

like a sundial in the shade
or the blade of a scissors
in plaster. I know you might

not even bring the tip
of your letter opener to this
tempting, international blue, airmail envelope

overflowing with good news. I know that I'm
a coward and crazy to ask
for another shot, but I gave

Brooklyn Bob your likeness
drawn with charcoal on boxer
shorts and warned about the red

highlights of your hair, your short
fuse. I'm coming down
with a fever that makes you lose

bits of memory in a labyrinth
of dreams that breed like clouds, day
or night, until the past turns

white and vaporous, so
please hurry.

Crawling Between Earth and Heaven

August in the stunned
aftermath of your tidal
moaning that ran, like the spirit
of our lovemaking, just ahead
of your uterus crashing
into itself for one night bleeding

into another. Your mother,
torn between the fear
of watching and the need
to participate, pivoted
away from the door to take
the full measure of your determined

suffering into the red, demilitarized
zone of her eyes, your arms draped
around my neck, the child
in your belly pressed
against the child in me,
waiting to curl

into you. Then, hunkered
almost to the floor, you launched
our upside-down, live
grenade into the cradle
of the midwife's hands, while the bloodless
flow of the Iraqi

war machine waved
Kuwaiti flags and Kalishnikovs
over the border, an immaculate
concept that delivered

and multiplied, richocheting
into born-again

arms deals with the Holy Land.
The afterbirth, like a wounded
war hero unwilling to quit
the theater of operations, breaks
from its cord. Doctor-on-call in combat
fatigues lifts his arm, like a surface-

to-air missile launcher,
into a surgical glove. Born in the usual
storm of mucous and blood, a chalky
miniature lies belly-down like a bandelero
across your breasts surrounded
by the midwife's exhaustion

and your mother wondering
out loud into the suddenly quiet
birthing corridor if anyone's
curious about the baby's
sex. March. It's mud season
in the united states of being

in love with the fine
motor skills of my daughter's
thumb and forefinger plucking a dog
hair from the rug, disgusted
with myself and everyone else
for permitting El Presidente numero

cuarenta y uno to sucker us
into a slaughter climaxed
with an independence-day display of every

smart piece of metal discharged
into the retreating backs of the current

stranger to democracy, liberating
them from themselves, and us from our thriving
reputation as losers. Let's
drag out the red
white and blue ice cream, crack

the sun roof and strap
the baby into a victory
spin around the new world
in our Japanese
minivan.

Jungle Gliders

I was kneeling with my daughter into a chaos
of frog-shaped jigsaw cutouts guaranteed
to coalesce into animal acrobats that range
the upper levels of South Asian jungles, when,
looking up into the Dragon Lizard's ribs spread
into wings pictured on the box that my son,
making bomber sounds, held
over my head, I remembered the roach that fell
out of the fist-size hole in the ceiling
of my first furnished room, almost
eighteen and kneeling
between your pale
knees in the air, mine dug into the heap
of coats and blankets that covered the concrete
carpet of my basement palace, where
we were struggling for warmth
and pleasure, when the gold-bellied
angel of retribution, like a miniature
landlord, dropped through the punch-drunk
hole in my character, through the onion-scented
fumes from the heater jammed in the window
and landed on your freckle we'd christened
The Third Eye. Watching the impossibly
thin legs, upside-down and flailing,
spinning the hard shell, my jungle-
gliding Paradise Tree Snake slid
out of you into the bedclothes. Your cupped hand
pulled me toward your tongue hovering
between your teeth, like the barely
visible eye of a Red-Tailed
Flying Squirrel, as if to will

our privacy and concentration
no matter what. Just as your other
hand splayed across the small
of my back nudged
me into you, the insect,
whose family tree had inhabited
every Eden, oasis, every four-star
constellation of food and drink,
righted itself and ran
like three little bodies portaging
an upturned canoe toward the secret
passageway of memory, where
I loved you when I wasn't running
on anger, an adolescent
ground predator, dogfaced
and tracking the family
blood into the trap
of my first poem. Is this
the Flying Lemur of Colugo, my daughter
wondered, reaching
for the upside-down creature, its claws
around a branch, sheltering a smaller
version of itself on its belly, the passenger
staring at the gecko
gliding toward tropical bark, where yellow-flowered
Spider Orchids trail out of ferns, like your hair
between my fingers, while we collided
and turned toward separate futures under the moonlit
shadow of the jet bearing Kennedy's body that
swept a million dreams into the ocean.

The Five Seasons

The Life and Times of My Last Idea

Einstein told Thomas Mann that he only
had one idea his whole life and you know

what that was. And what it must have been
to be sitting in Princeton sipping tea

listening to Albert
chew the expatriate corner of his moustache

watching Tom scribble on paper scraps pulled
out of the arcane recesses of his dark

three-piece suit and wonder
out loud if he'd ever get around

to that novel he started thirty years ago. Don't
worry, said Einstein, it will come around to you.

As Mann slowly pushed the pretzel
basket across the table with a callous-

studded middle finger, the tea kettle
whistling downstairs brings us four decades into this

snow-covered extravaganza with moonlight. The first
December morning is minutes away; icicles

like transparent swordfish hang from the eaves
and you sleep diagonally

across the bed, one foot on the pillow, one
toe raised like a torch. One minute

we're making love, the next
the phone rings and rings and the answering machine

answers in your voice, deep and tinted
with a little laughter as the dog

barks and the flashing orange
lights of a plow set the room on fire.

Ornamental Agony of December

I rake my fingernails across a white
flecked beard that conceals a renegade

innermost self, that berserk boy
who dreamt of lizards climbing

out of a fistful of mulberries,
who stood his ground and hurled

his hundred pounds through glass, who broke
down in the corner of the emergency

room into a red-eyed
heap, shards glittering

his fingertips. The nurse,
pulling a curtain around the bed,

took my pulse and whispered, Don't do this
to them ever again. I remember

her fingers on my wrist, searching
for a heartbeat she could take

the measure of, the hard line
of her eyebrows frowning

at the body trying to dig
through the mattress, maybe fall

forever through the world's mystery, sleep
through adolescence and what

would pass for adulthood. When an ice dam
broke over the doorway last night and hammered me

into the new snow, I saw myself
as that boy running at a window and tried

to reach for him before he fell,
but I heard the machine

of my parents' arguing grinding
in the background that opened

my eyes to the sliver
of moon stuck in a cobalt sky,

lying there like a middle-aged
snow angel with a pulsing

bump on my forehead, until my daughter
opened the door for the desperate

dog, who licked snow from my chin
while he relieved himself on an iced-over

ornamental. Then she grabbed
a fistful of snow with mischief

in her eye, and I let her sail one
before I dived at her.

Passover Mud

This morning the blood-soaked
muzzle of my steel-jawed
mutt led me to where the spring

overflow and the torn
carcass of a fawn wrapped
over a strand of barbwire

met a stream plunging into a tree-
studded pond. I stuck the black
nose into the gore. With fist

and elbow, knee and boot, screaming
I punished him, who stuck
to my side all the way to this desk,

where he crawled underneath, twitched
and ran headlong through the mystery
of dog sleep. Someday, my neighbor's

son will wake before dawn and take
his rifle down to the beaver pond to get
their attention for a little population

control, as he calls it, and catch
my dog running a deer in his sight, slowly
squeeze the trigger and drag

the body back to my door, come in
for coffee and talk about the international
conspiracy of Washington bureaucrats,

communists, Japanese
manufacturers and the Pope controlling
the flow of money, controlling the weather.

Night on Bear Mountain

I climbed the firetower
in the rain, the leash
wrapped three times
around my wrist, a hundred
pounds of canine
hesitation in the flashlight beam
leading the way. I lifted

his paws to a window in the lookout
and watched his nose twitch,
his eye fix on a squirrel skittering
across spruce needles and cones
that bobbed in its wake. I set him down
growling at the wind lashing
the rain toward the next

mountain, like the shiver
that ran the length of wet fur. Dog-
envious, I scraped the light
across trees that housed
mice and chickadees, searching

for what it was like to sleep
all night and wake in time
to get away from the bad guy.
I confessed to the invisible
allies of insomniacs that my wife
wants a baby and I'm not sure
what the skinflint I work for

really wants for his penny, or why
I came here ready to jump.

When my flashlight found a birch,
its bark peeled and waving
like the flag of winter
surrendering, a voice in the tower
said, No one ever killed himself

walking his dog. That dovetails
with my experience, I answered
into the tailwind of the Great Dane
pussyfooting down the steps.
Two dozen feet from the ground,

his right front paw slipped
into space off a slick riser. I held
my breath and the leash tighter
at the prospect of the two of us
tumbling end over end, and yearned
to change a diaper or pick another
fight with my boss, to forgive my cousin's

stab in the back and write my way
into one more corner. A pickup truck's
spotlight from below swept the tower
until it found the red eyes
of my companion, who genetically

dislikes light shined in his face,
and men in hats and uniforms
made more sinister by a dashboard
glow. I imagined climbing
back to the penthouse and screaming,
Top of the world, Ma, but the dog

bit through the leash, then leapt
at the windshield. While my eyes
were closed, the truck lurched
and he landed in a bed of hay. The ranger
tossed him a baloney and mustard sandwich,
dressed me down, then drove
the pair of us off the mountain.

Parable of the First Frost

I have a friend who got so angry
at the woman he was going to marry

he broke her rocking chair
over his own head. Our bellies full
of the lazy last minutes of summer,

he told me this before a mutt paused
by farmer Taber's gristly skull, cradled

and snoring in a cleavage of birch leaves.
The camel-colored hound, nonchalant and looking
right through our curiosity, raised

the drawbridge of his hind leg in the slickest
motion since Moses parting the waters

and doused the old skin. My friend, who loves
a geezer smiling in his sleep, dogs
and a good fiddle tune, took his

out of the case, lifted his chin
whiskers with the bow, and swore

he'd never again let a woman get
his goat. Just as she snuck in from behind,
covering his eyes, and whispering

into his ears going crimson, farmer Taber
shot out of a hole in the covered bridge

and backstroked into the sun going down
on the lake. Before long,
we had most of the town slapping

each other's backs, thighs bobbing,
yelling at the echo over the water,

stomping night crawlers as they swung
their partners under the moonlit bickering
of red and yellow leaves in the midnight

breeze that made us shiver, lock our doors
and not come out until April.

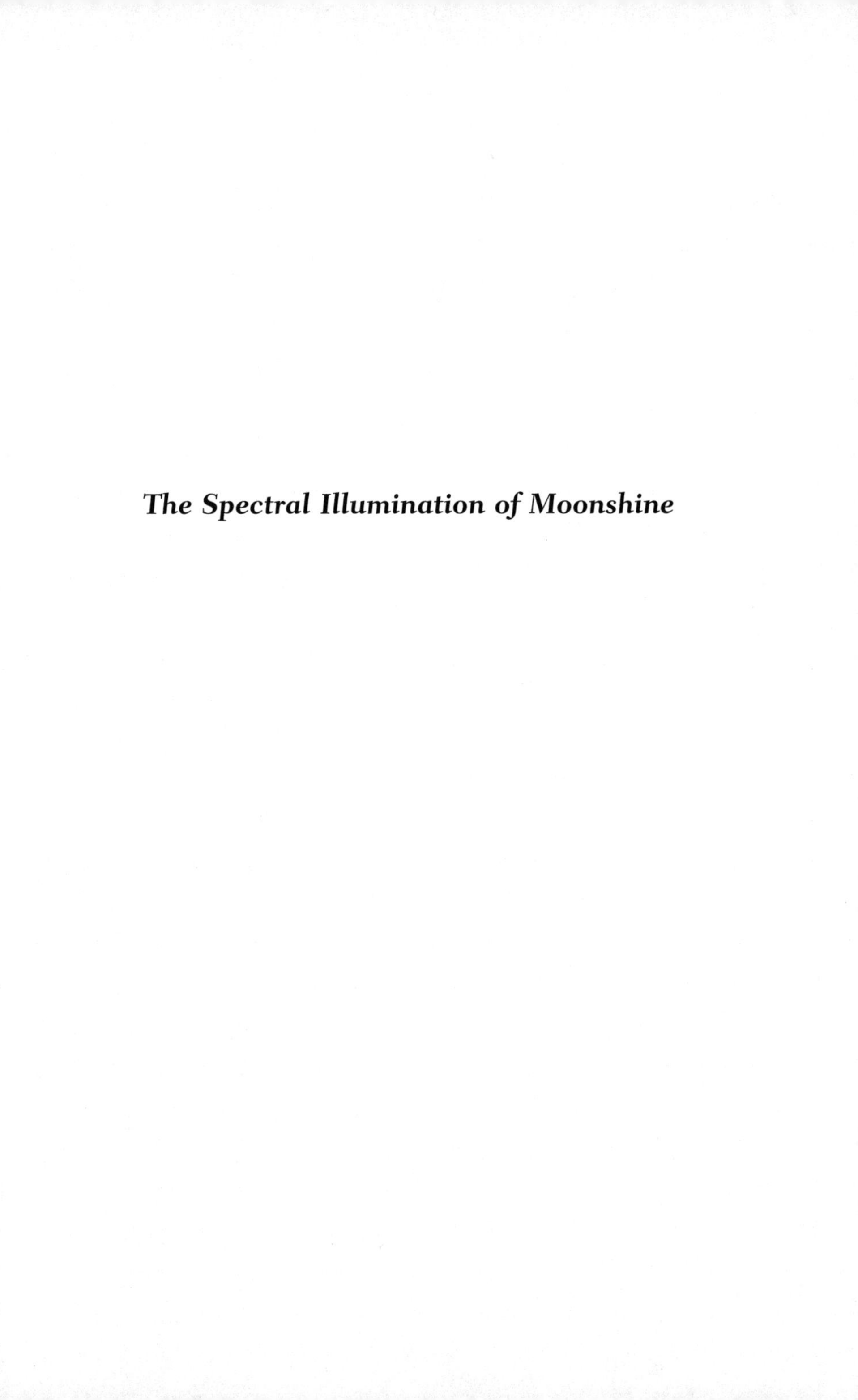

The Spectral Illumination of Moonshine

The Afterlife

Gauze branches of a palo verde enter stage right
and freeze before an iron balustrade
secured in a stream surrounding a plaque

rising out of desert scrub, riveted to the door
of a pyramid, milk-white as the eye of a newborn,
where Governor W. P. (Pee Wee) Hunt, his wife,

his grandfather, an albino pair of dobermans
on either side of his half-sister, are holding court. They
invite you in out of the turquoise

of the Phoenix Zoo, scalloped at the edges,
like the postcard you slipped down your pants
behind the stuffed zebra in a pink sombrero. Walking

backwards out of swinging doors, you daydreamed
being born out of wedlock. Given
minutes to pack, you took to your heels with an armload

of two-toed sloths, armadillo, and beaver—between a sunburn
eating a sausage and a bystander winding his watch,
and that banker yawning whose secretaries in bikinis

gather into a mob. But you strip one lumber jacket here, one
    belt
buckle there, and they let you escape their embarrassment
and disappear. Into the pyramid, the half-sister

takes you aside to worship crates of porcupines
multiplying in the library, flamingoes
with the run of the place. The incense is so

out of this world, she whispers over the clipped
ears of her pale bodyguards drooling on her slippers, that I
am going to have my way with everyone. Although the wife

understands how the half-sister might be so inclined,
she blames the ancient swamp cooler beyond the musk
ox exhibit. Oh don't be alarmed, she reads from her guide book

whisking you around the parlor, by the glass eye installed
in the governor's socket. I was scattering ammonia
from a window one of those stillborn

afternoons Teddy Roosevelt was out practicing his gunboat
diplomacy, when old Pee Wee just happened by with the half-
sister wrapped around his forearm and looked up. We

don't talk about it, he rasps, looking down at you—an upside-
down warrior angel in a waxed moustache and an ice cream
suit dangling from a chandelier. If I fall on you

and it gets inflamed, I'll just wear a patch, period. Heck,
it was only a little matter of me being in the wrong light
at the wrong time, wasn't it? Funnier things

have happened, she reads from her book. True,
he replies. His grandfather agrees. The dogs bark.
And they were silent for the rest of their lives.

The man listening to "Don't
You Know I Care, or Don't
You Care To Know" is in love
with the woman wrapped in a sheet
almost asleep on the other side
of the radio, Venetian blinds
cutting them both into chalk
and charcoal. This bearded man smoking
in the buff, on the floor, his arms
folded tight to his belly,
looks up at the tobacco-
stained breath forging

a shaft of snakeskin that ripples
across the ceiling. His big toe
tapping into the air
conditioned breeze, he foresees
his genital flesh turning
into a withering
shadow that hangs itself

in low branches over the entrance
to a village where cattle graze
and drink. The woman—passing off
the summer lightning of his despair
for a fugitive vision before sleep—flies
out of this world to a hovering
female figure. Their shoulder blades
circle and touch. Mourning doves
echo the moonlight
over a gorge. A beaver slaps
its tail against the still

surface, porcupines prowl
like night hags visiting
the local witch, and the cool
tangle of snakes flickers in the twigs
that lead him to a Sunday morning in the dark
outpost of the balcony, where he relieves
himself of a stream of consciousness
over the railing, over the wind chimes
and potted plants of neighbors
drifting in the sacred dream.

Aura, Cry, Fall and Fit

I hold my twin brother's head
in my skirt on the cool oak floor—the cut
was slight; the seizure was not—until he recovers
enough for me to leave then return
to bathe his wound. We come from a proud and ancient
line of winemakers who spent centuries collecting

antique mansions—not so haunted that just anyone
wandering in could put their hand on what kept them
on edge or slightly aroused. We grew up above it all
on a third floor, but it was I, rifling
a steamer trunk of diaries, who found the concealed
occupation of this place was to kill a relative

on Christmas, Easter or a name day. Before the grand mal
but after listening to Uncle Constantine's history
of our family, Karl looked right through me—I remember
looking around for a mirror—forcing me, just nineteen,
to thoroughly blush, as if crossing an ocean and the apron
of the stage of our childhood at Uncle's invitation
had divorced us from our sibling selves and turned us—

black-haired, green-eyed and virgins—
into lovers. Over Russian salad and armagnac,
Constantine was about to, as he put it, "finish
my education," when Karl abruptly left the table.
"In 1823, one of your ancestors—who built this house
out of cathedral windows and beams arching like the limbs
of a praying mantis—seduced his daughter, who gave birth
to a son, who suffocated his father, also his grandfather,
in front of his mother, also his sister. These apparitions

turn paintings upside-down in the corridors." "Nonsense,"
said Aunt Zenia, his third wife, who, at table
the next morning, announced that Constantine
had died in his sleep. Karl, looking at himself
in his boots' high polish, said, "They came for him
on his name day; they will come for me,
and they will find you, Cassandra, on your toes
trimming the Christmas tree, unless we gather

our forces and speak to them in a way
they'll never forget." Hand-in-hand
with an uncorked Montrachet, a gouda and apples,
we climbed through a crush of family portraits,
their faded, cracked, indifferent eyes pushing us
up then down on a quilt Karl spread over our uncle's

oriental. We shaped a man with apples for eyes, a round
of cheese for a belly, lit candles and lay
next to him and drank. Ashes in the grate
were stirring in a draft; the thin light
of dusk poured cobalt through the leaded glass.
He threw my dress over the head of our soft
sculpture, entered me, and we fell, like a fairy tale,
into a trance, all I remember… then a young man

dressed in full fig, a wig, lace at the wrist
and a short beard appeared from behind
a tapestry. The eyes of the cheeseman
rolled under the bed as we dived
for the quilt to take cover. He lifted
his coattails over his thighs, sat down
and drank right from the bottle. "You have been,"
he said, wiping wine off his lips with a finger,

"misinformed about this house. I wish to clarify
a few details." Could I pass my hand
through the bulge of his Adam's apple, I wondered;
did he want me to? "Years ago," he went on,
looking into the quartet of eyes steaming
under the quilt, "our mutual relation was out
for his morning ride through the trees. His horse

reared, and to the peasant who found him he seemed
no longer among the living. A brood of doctors
pronounced him 'in a trance,' though, knowing
little about it and caring less, they left him
to the devices of Sister Madeleine, who washed,
sang and talked to him late into the night.
One evening, after several years, reading
aloud from Revelations, she looked up to find him

staring. A moment passed, and then he fell on her.
She ran for Sister Evangeline, who looked gingerly
through a crack, mesmerized by the man on his back asleep.
She advised Madeleine to confess her dream. Instead,
Madeleine ran, poor and without prospects, past the age
of marriage, past the village of her childhood, past
her parents, old and on their knees in a pew—running

like a poet's ghost trying to free itself of voices,
until, destitute and nearly broken, she returned
as a nurse, no longer God's bride, to bathe the endless
film of sleep and trim the beard that spread
like frost grapes out of the sea
of his steady breathing. She looked up again—
a few years had passed—on his name day. He
looked back. She said that she had loved him

half-alive, that she was no longer a nun, if only
he could stay awake. This time
when she went for Evangeline, the Sister
stormed the room, a flurry of anger, derision,
and it wasn't until months later—when she could put
a glass and her ear to Madeleine's belly and hear

the persistent, tidal rhythms of a child's heart—
that she apologized, so mortified she made a pilgrimage
to Bethlehem and never returned. Madeleine
gave suck and the rudiments of an education
to Christina in the hospital room, which they rarely left,
caring for him for nearly thirteen years. One evening,
Madeleine was about to read. He stirred, she ran,
and he chased her down the hill to a fountain,
where she threw herself into the turbulence flowing

out of the marble-green mouths of tigers.
He rescued her and they talked: 'I've been
sleeping for days.' 'You've been sleeping for years
and we have a child named Christina because
you fell on me.' 'If I've lost years, I'll take
the child for what I've wasted, but you
must leave.' He groomed Christina like an idiot-wife
or an idolized mistress. She had your eyes and artistic
fingers and the dark spot you both share
below your knee. She saw no one else, no room

but this, and when their desires became urgent,
he had his way with her. He summoned
the old nurse back because of his wife-daughter's
inability to raise a son, who, reaching
his eighteenth year, his father about to die,
was to become lord of the house and a wealthy man.

The nurse laid the truth before the boy. That night,
after dispatching three generations with two serene

strokes of a razor, he threw himself from a parapet
into the warm air. At the wake, the nurse looked
beyond the two bodies lying in state to the still
figure of her grandson and begged the priest, 'Don't
bury this boy. Like his father in a trance
for nearly twenty years, he's still alive.'"

A small meteor crashed into the churchyard. The town,
forced to make repairs, found Uncle Constantine
clutching himself, surrounded by fantastic carvings
lining the coffin. Aunt Zenia, who went quietly

in an asylum outside of Prague, willed the house
and everything in it to me and Karl, who,
like a superstitious child, had it shipped
in pieces and reassembled near Salt Lake City, where
we entertain an occasional stranger.

Passover in the French Quarter

Angel of vengeance comes in low over Bourbon Street
Takee-Outee. The tabasco-stained ceiling drips
its message over impaled blackened shrimp,

voodoo chicken, and matzo balls buried in rice
and red beans. His wings folded into the prayer
shawl of an old believer, bearded, wearing a skullcap,

and out for a stroll, he stops before
the pearl-shaped double doors of Oyster Heaven, where sweet
intoxication rises out of bricks and almost every elder

statesman in the quarter has gratefully
watered down the mortar, looking up at neon
"shuck 'em, suck 'em, and eat 'em raw," boogie-shuffling

down the block to salty blues and the twang
of country rock, past the pecan praline confectioner's revolving
cauldron of goo blazing in the sunset. Crossing over,

he nods Good shabbas to the female impersonator with
the forty-days-and-forty-nights physique, who dips
her torso-of-Apollo tuchas down for a cannonball. Skin

to win, she whispers, pointing out the shaded
promenade of a jazz saloon, where—in a plastic bullfrog,
hard-boiled egg, and bone of the paschal lamb barrage—

a juggler with a mezzuzah tattooed on his back recites
the story of Moishe-from-the-Bible's glory, while a nun
on the next corner holding out a tambourine

lifts the angel's wallet from his greatcoat
as he passes. Unable to find any firstborn Egyptian males,
he runs around giving Jews their walking papers

to flee the city, then falls like a zombie into the aisle
of a great liquor store, decanters
of many colors spinning his head around. Waxing

philosophical, he tucks a jar of vodka-soaked
jalapenos into his coat and flies
into a rain cloud that never stops until the last

sequin flickers in the swirling waters, like the sabbath
candlelight of a voodoo shrine hidden behind
an ancient magnolia, extinguished in the prying

fingertips of the wind.

Villanelle of the Crucified and the Risen Christ

Almost identical, nearly Siamese; more than twice
the tongue of Mother Church, imbedded firmly in a rock,
has preached the crucified and the risen Christ.

After the crowns backed out of the manger, little brother quietly
fell like another star in Father's eye into Mother's.
Call us irrational, merely conspirators: more than twice

was brother Jesus taken for brother Christ: he, a knee-slapping,
    feisty
rabblerouser; and me, a rabbi, a real thinker, always turning
the other cheek of the crucified and the risen Christ.

We walked slowly on my shoulders across the water, forty days
    and nights,
applauded our Holy Father's repartee with the fallen angel's
violent, almost identical speech. More than twice

as hungry as ever in our lives, Beelzebub's surprising
illusion of bread rising out of cactus
almost reached the stupified and the suspicious Christ.

Under the table at the last supper, little brother gave me crumbs
on his fingers dipped in wine. I lifted him down into the
    outcome.
Almost responsible, nearly at peace, more than twice
alive I reappeared and preached a crucified and a risen Christ.

The Dark Gold Hummock of Desire

Under flame-yellow grosbeaks swaying in the high
candelabra of branches against a black

April cloud, a two-story circle of overflowing
slurry tanks surrounded me

and my shovel shoplifting from widow Manosh's
manure pile, while a cacophony of escapees,

their beaks freckled brown from pecking
hard yellow kernels out of the litter

of turban-shaped cow pies, brought the neighborly
Manosh toting her double-chambered

fowling piece to get a whiff
of what was cooking. Last poacher

on this dung pile came away—she ran her tongue
over her lower lip—with an orchidectomy

for his trouble. Before I could inquire
into this simultaneously

lush and frightening term, she pressed
her forefinger to the blue steel

trigger, then, with the other hand, reached
between my legs and squeezed, not

daintily but not too hard, while she
asked if I would like to break

into a fresh apple pie and some coffee.
She released

the weapon and her grip on the consecutive
sets of twins and the stillborn child

in my future. I stuck the blade
of my shovel into the dark gold

hummock. Aren't you the poet living
in the neighbor's corn crib? she said,

musing over the broken
eyelet in my boot as she pulled it off

in her mud room. What's
an orchidectomy, I asked, unbuttoning her smoky

blue sweater. After we've eaten, she answered,
everything there is to eat and you still

have an appetite, then I'll watch you
look it up, and you'll tell me.

The Ayatollah of I Told You So

Knowing the reach of that dog, I told you not to leave
your four-alarm chili on the stove. You swore even my
thieving mutt wasn't that stupid. His black nose burned
on the bottom of the pot wouldn't heal for weeks. What

did I tell you? Chorus: I told you so. After dog
methane kept your nostrils dreaming the clip-clop
of a horse cop trotting away from steam
off a stately pile, your daybreak revelation

of luck running through your lucky veins
made me frank: keep your unrepentant
blowhole out of our hard-earned booty stuffed
into the band-aid tin or I'll bite it off.

You grinned, biting into the dog swimming
in mustard, then your nag dumped the jockey
at the starting gate, while I sprinkled
your bet like confetti into your beer. What

did I tell you? Chorus: I told you so. Your five
o'clock shadow seemed so despondent, I said it might
feel better to turn me into the first lady
of a poem so the world would know how I tease

the hairs of your imagination into a peak, but you wormed
your fingers into mine and pulled me out of my back seat
driver's soliloquy. Let's find a sugar maple,
you murmured between my knees, and wrap ourselves

like possum tails around a branch. The car phone
beeped—the receiver wilted in my palm. It was God's

gift to birth control, my mother,
wanting specifics, while she jabbed her cuticle

with an orangewood stick. I told her you were a fly-
by-night sperm bank without a nickel in your pants.
And what do you think she told me? Doris, don't
tell your mother she never told you so.

The Spectral Illumination of Moonshine

In heaven that night the moths—
pale green bits of glass—and mosquitos
as bloodthirsty as I've ever seen
haunted my feet washed in moonlight.

I shot the breeze with God's
little entourage who cleaned the place and kept the books.
I-am-that-I-am Himself materialized out of the stuff
heavenly thrones are made of. He was a pot-bellied

stove with a lighthouse of hair yellow
as squash meat sticking out of the infinite
wisdom of each ear. Into mine
an angel whispered that certain formalists

believe moonlight began with an itch and a shooting star
of wax flickering into the void. God was naked
as a sheered ram, sheepdip-
pink and glistening. He wore

a multitude of corns and varicose veins like
string beans. To my surprise
he wasn't circumcised, his fingernails so long
they curved into pinwheels. His ancient

tits sinking into armpits gave off a glowing aromatic
haze that disappeared behind the dark side
of his shoulder blades. Like an old miser squinting
through venetian blinds, he looked right through me,

gummed his ivory grin into place and said,
My son, I thought I

told you to despise Daughter
of the American Revolution types, who grow

as fungus grows between the toes of traditional prosody.
Their only subject is not the subject they subject us to.
Am I getting warm? And the choir of angels'
sweet hosannas sang, "Yes, Lord, You're Getting Warm"

and that put him to sleep like a lullaby. Day broke. The wind
rushed from the Holy Seat, where He woke and said, I dreamt
your wife ran off with a Seventh Day Adventist large
dog breeder. I thought I told you

to shave your moustache, stay off the phone, and love her
till death do you part, starting
at the little bones of her feet and spiralling
upward out of the vortex of your own exuberant,

epic narcissism. What's got into you? Why
are you standing in heaven when you look like hell?
Don't tell me, I've already heard the ructating,
big-bang, rack-and-screw denouement

of your story. Think how the errors
of your ways reflect my image. You're not
a sideshow geek or a chicken-faced
upstate novelist picking hairs out of a butter dish. So

don't say I love you less than that eternal
bitch of a neighbor who won't share
his wife, or swear a perpetual
silent but deadly fart on that sweet-talking

lawyer who screwed you good when you were
down for the count. You're not embalmed

and lying in state. But when you are
I might have work for you, dancing

on the head of a pin or spoonfeeding
ambrosia to the occasional
hummingbird. By Christ, you may
rely on my word. Who's next?

Ghost Wrestling

"I will not let thee go,
except thou bless me."

Genesis 32:26

In the Cloud Chamber

Weightless in the shower, I was sailing
on my own adolescent
current of song, my voice
breaking into suds and spray
when the stall door cracked
open to a slice
of my father sliding the knot
in his tie toward his throat
asking was it all right with me
if he remarried. Can't hear,
I shouted, soap in my eyes.
His new shoe's perfect
shine took a giant step
backward into the billowing
steam. Years later, I told
my four year old in the tub,
I'm leaving your mother, then
asked if he understood I wasn't
leaving him. He left
his wind-up scuba diver sputtering,
stepped into a towel and without a word
closed the mirror-backed door
in my dripping face. My reflection
distorted in the chrome
doorknob turned counter-clockwise.
My red-eyed boy returned
an angel of vengeance in pajamas,
threw a punch then another
I caught in flight. We tumbled
to the bath mat. He cried,
kneed and scratched, his entire

being flailing at mine. Seven years
of weekends and holidays into the future,
dreaming I'm on my knees at the foot
of the porcelain throne clipping my dead
father's toenails, the white
crescents growing back
as I go, the sound of bathwater
lapping turns me around to the skinny
frame of my son afloat, raging
at someone he can't see, calling out
the garbled words of a child in sleep,
the steam rising.

Amber

Two men lowering long-necked bottles
from their mouths looked down
at the lightning-shattered

tulip tree, the late
afternoon sun at their backs
burning the constellation

of their shadows
into the pale cadaver.
The bearded one claimed

every friend he ever depended on
wandered into an answering
machine or skindived

into an uncompromising
marital bliss. The other spat
at what he saw slithering

through the gutted
astronomy of the tree, running
his fingers where his hair

used to curl around them
and confessed every friend
he ever trusted betrayed him.

They drove the amber
empties into the spongy
heartwood, kicked

the timber down a mudslide
into the backyard ravine,
slid and rolled

after it, laughing
so hard they couldn't speak, to bury
the glass-hearted tree

under waterlogged armloads
of last year's leaves, until,
submerged in debris and muck

like Cain and Abel born midlife
out of primeval goo, they grabbed
exposed roots and saplings to boost

each other into the world
of wives and two little
boys throwing sticks

at each other, who watched
their mudcaked fathers
materialize and screamed.

Dear Mike

My half of the closet floor is a sideshow
of shoes I've tucked

into cartons of knickknacks
and clutter, skipping town because

of a job or marriage gone sour
in the cab of a rented truck.

Sometimes, I'll slide
into a boot missing buckles

I wore into great Uncle Moishe's
secret swamp, his medicine

ball belly chasing blue-eyed wings.
When your estranged daughter phoned,

my wife you never met
hauled me by the feet

out of sleep to relay news
of your heart attack. I pulled the chain

on the closet light, dropped
to my knees and tossed

flapping soles of loafers
over my shoulder, frantic to find

oxblood cordovans, their tongues
twisted into the dry

scream you shipped me off
to college in after throwing

a hook to my chin—trying to sift
through layers of tire-tread

sandles, threadbare walkers, spikes
I never used, gunboats that danced

the hokie-pokie; searching
for a clue to our unresolved

arguments or years of visits terminating
in mutual relief, to the adolescent

joy when I grew
into your spit-shined, tricolor

wingtips. Together,
we stepped into the hushed

nursing home, where Moishe
held my cheeks like the pages

of a prayer book he read
to his flock, who joined him

in chanting "Little Mike"
over and over, embarrassing

us into a silence we grew
accustomed to after my older

brother stepped off the balcony
of his wife's infidelity

into the surf. I held his high-top
running shoes like conch shells

over her ears, until you pulled up
in a brushfire of disbelief and told me

to drop the sneakers and pretend
they never existed. Yesterday,

your wife, whispering
into the hospital pay phone, said

you remained incommunicado, but if I
wanted to grovel and beg in a letter,

she'd put it into your hands
when the time was right.

I keep going back to
when I was four and zigzagging

a crayon across white
patent leather you were wearing, buried

in the sports page, while Mom
finished dressing for a summer dance.

Your thumbs hooked around suspenders,
holding a smile back, you swore

you'd wear them even if she
didn't approve. When I refused

to apologize, she marched me
off to bed without supper.

I could hear an argument brewing
through the floor until you appeared

to tuck me in, apples and hunks
of cheese falling out of your cummerbund.

When you left the house for good,
you forgot the shoes. Your grandchildren

think of you as a constellation
of anecdotes: driving me to jail

for setting a field on fire; the fart
exploding when I stretched for a pretend

spanking across your lap; the after-dinner
cigar you let me puff until I turned green.

The oldest remembers a man in bathing trunks
who spun him around in an inner tube

until he cried uncle. The youngest,
building a pyramid of shoes in the closet,

wonders if you have a secret hiding place
filled with guns and dynamite.

I don't tell him that every time
I remember the woman

waving a miniature flag
through our old neighborhood—her face

like torn and crumpled paper, stopping to scream
at an invisible traitor—and the porchlit

summer night you gave her a glass
of tea she smacked against yours,

the blue numbers on her wrist
visible through the screen door,

every time I imagine you touching
those numbers like a bruise, tucking her

under your arm and rocking
back and forth to music only you could hear,

I want to crash through the screen
of every stranger you helped

through a chain of strangers, every intricate
business deal you hinted at,

every brushoff or receiver
hurried into its cradle—crash and land

on a bus to Montreal with you and a bag
of salami sandwiches and tell dumb jokes

and brag until you doze off, then I'll slip
to the floor and weave our shoelaces

together into a knot so complicated,
so tight, you could never untangle it.

Moment of Vaulted Chambers

He was nude, but for the tear gland
of bathing trunks and a profile

of Mars on his middle finger, his
belly laughing at the blue

edge of the pool I splashed
into sunlight onto the bone

white scar where the muscle over his heart
disappeared in a World War II stateside

training mission. I followed him under the high
tiled ceilings of the Turkish bath,

steaming into the calloused
grip of the masseuse, worried, at thirteen,

about getting a hard-on. Out
of the showers, into the grill, we shared

a slab of burnt steak buried in a hail storm
of shattered garlic—loving

the freedom of that laugh, the high
gloss of his teeth and the knotted

towel that never fell from his waist.
Like a flock of crows

I could sometimes see over the next town,
his business grew into distance. For every new

year of life, every nickel secreted in the safe
deposit of memory, he climbed another

step into the cool, stone, faraway
look of wealthy men. In the dashboard glow

his genital key ring twirled and bobbed in a slow
curve through tall, shadowy

warehouse stacks of mahogany, ash
and wormy chestnut. Mother left his body

for another but pursued his fuck-
the-children attitude to amuse herself

and her companion, leaving a snake-
filled cradle on his welcome mat, a sign,

the note said, of things to come. And when
a hearse pulled up before sunrise

he didn't get the funny
part of the joke. He married the ice

queen of greed and country club
repartee and retired to an even richer

state of being. A golf ball
ash tray, wine and the platinum aura

of Florida framing closed
venetian blinds—I knew

that he knew he wasn't safe, collecting
jade or relaxing

in the coconut shade, his ex-wife still
bringing him to his off-white

knees before the bench, he who once made
a miraculous landing and lived

long enough to disinherit
the narrator. You know how it is: you try

to write the field guide to dangerous fathers
staring over spectacles at your own

little ones trying to figure you, sitting up
all day in bed, a bearded

heartbeat surrounded
by a no-man's land of crumpled bone

white paper, and you pull one
then the other

up over the stillborn mess
and confess to the weevil gnawing

on the muscle pumping
life through your nearly forty-

year-old skin that you need to know
how a father—before the High

Holy Days trade sin and guilt
for prayer and hunger—how a father,

possibly in need himself of even this
daydreamy variation on the theme of son

willing to carry on everything
but the family business of refusing

to forgive, could crumple
you like a parking ticket,

drive over it and pull away. Young
and old from both sides try hard

to help. One of them
left this message on the machine: If

the son of Abraham held a razor
to his father's balls, would God

himself step in and pull his wrist back?

The New Confessions

I had an almost famous friend who broke
into a Parisian library wearing purple
from his sneakers to his mask. Living it up
on a genius grant, he slithered out a window
he unlatched during business hours
with a first edition of Stevens'
Harmonium tucked into the business end
of his pleated pants. He said the thought
that no sullen or needy expatriate soul
bothered to steal it all those years
had wormed its way into his blood stream.
I told him if he committed the Stevens to my
perpetual care, I'd crawl in and out
of the library windows of this world
for him. Shifting a smoke to the other
side of his face, he counseled me to focus
on my break shot—before you and your wet dream
tear another hole in the cloth and the bartender
kicks us both out before we finish our beers. And how
could anyone stroke a cue while wearing
lace-up brown shoes that looked like injured
turds, anyway? He delivered this barrage
only weeks before he took back his half
of our friendship, twenty years

after I materialized in my best friend
from high school's doorway, where his
pupil occupied the peephole, then he
opened up to behold me holding a clear,
elbow-length veterinarian's glove almost
choked with bull testicles accompanied

74

by a red-haired vet holding another.
Now a psychiatric social worker in pepper
and salt whiskers down to his innie,
the companion to the ups and downs
of my adolescence eyed me through a wire-rimmed
aura of remove that never wavered, while his bride
lectured about the inner life of the inner city
they were trying to rescue. For breakfast,
we dined on scrambled eggs and balls, while the vet
and I—a divorcee and a fellow traveler—reminisced
about a raccoon stew we'd concocted
from a carcass a farmer had left in the snow
outside her trailer. Before she and I drove off
to fall for the same vegetarian paralegal,
my old friend asked would I mind
if he drove the surviving glove
to his clinic. Charmed by the idea of polled
Hereford glands making an entrance into the inner
sanctum of urban mental health, I called to hear
how it went. His bride blurted that she
had filed for divorce, it was all
my fault, and rammed the receiver
into the affirmative action of what became
my current recurring dream. In it,
I'm speeddialing a defunct friend's
unlisted number that sets off
a recording telling me to stop
monopolizing the message with non sequiturs
from Mother Goose and Martin Heidegger, or
at the beep I'll be electrocuted. The dial tone
inflates into my aromatherapist accusing
me of thinking like a long-distance call
that interrupts itself with a conference call

from two former friends, who agree to go
halvesies on a contract to take me out
of this dream. But how will I find the Dead
Friendship Office where I can sift
through the limbo of lost companions
if I'm awake? How will I find a coconut
cream pie, mocks the shrink who shrinks
into a tail and fur while traveling
hand over hand across the revolving
blades of a ceiling fan to drop an ampule
of fragrance that breaks
into my dream with a smoky roomful of bored
friends of friends no longer friends
in its wake, who press me
into a corner booth for quarters
to feed the eight ball. I charge
the gauntlet of upturned palms,
grab a cue out of the purple
hand of my old shadow, and pole-vault
to the ceiling for a whirling
tete-a-tete with the simian shrink, who
unleashes his own musk and sprinkler system,
screeching, When your checkbook balance
plummets to meet your self-image, introduce
a little oil of stinkweed
to your hairy oxters. Call me next
year if you need a refill.

Rapid Transit, July 1955

The pale headlight
charged the ravine
overrun with carrion
flowers, bull thistle
and broken bottles. It
stopped on my brother's
dime. A white-haired
woman in a veil disembarked,
and while the yellow train
lurched under the bridge
to come around for the return,
we transported our mischief
to the other track, where
the conductor chased us
upstairs to the street and
swore he would call the police
if he caught us. We turned
to find ourselves face-to-face
with the veiled woman. Her
nearly transparent skin
reeked of lavender. Pointing
over the railing at my brother's
dime, squashed and shiny, she
told us that her father
had kept silver dollars
in a cabinet almost
as high as the ceiling; that
once a week she'd climbed
a couch and a bookshelf
to steal one. She gave a coin
to each of us. We put them

on the track shaded
by the bridge, where we could
hardly read the word Liberty
splashed across the hair
of the woman in profile,
then climbed back to join
our companion. But she
was gone and so, after the train
disappeared into haze,
was our prize, though we searched
until it was long past
time to go, then ran into the
arms of our parents' fury waiting
with supper and a strap to hear
what had kept us.

Against Friendship

I came between what my former
friend called his "weakness"
and the woman in question, when,

despite his warning to keep
driving while negotiating
her neck of the northern bog, I

didn't hesitate to drop
out of nowhere, accompanied
by wife and baby, onto her

bathroom rug to change
a loaded diaper. You betrayed me,
he declared over the phone

when I returned to the States.
Didn't I tell you it would wreck
everything? There's nothing

more to say. Except, I said,
when ex-President Reagan was reminiscing
with a talk-show priestess about bartering

arms for hostages, he was speaking
on my behalf when he confessed, "I guess
we committed a boner." Though I couldn't

guess what harm our visit had brought,
I listened to the half-life
of his laughter disintegrate into the fiber

optic silence connecting us, fraying

around his core belief that all his friends
inevitably let him down. I told him not to write

me off, that no friend had ever loved him
as much, but he never heard that. He was rasping
into the receiver: You know the alibi

she laid on her jealous mate? That you
and I were lovers in the Socratic mold.
Too bad I'm the last to know, I said. Yeah,

he said, and too bad her husband broke
her ribs and two of her oldest boy's teeth
minutes after you evacuated

the premises. His eyes control me, wrote
his Nora Barnacle out of the blue
from her desk overlooking the mackerel

cannery, its incense faintly emanating
from the fragile onionskin, who'd never,
she confessed, had an orgasm before

our mutual friend and his magic wand
materialized. She said, I know he's busy
denouncing both of us

to half the world. I know he wants
all my sisters on a platter, maybe
my dad's sisters and their vows

of silence to boot. But if I could backfloat
day and night in the wild schemes
swirling around his scalp's

red glow, I would. And I'd still
want to take you down the backroads around
my favorite ruins and oyster beds.

Although you've erased the pleasure
you took in each other laughing
into the sun that seemed to swim

in place as you leaned endless
evenings on the fence you baptized
The Wailing Wall with your swords

crossed, I want you to know
your friendship carved its initials
into my life. Perched on stairs cut

into the hill above the alternating
current of your voices, I handrolled one
after another and smoked to the music

of my name, hearing it rise, richochet
and break.

Ghost Wrestling

The memory of holding
my ground in the wind

tunnel of my father's
anger dived clawfirst

into the morning I was
skating through fog

in snowshoes down a slow
curve, daydreaming across

time zones into my son's
dream of a long-haired

dog leaping for a stick
in the ravine behind

his mother's piece
of California, when one

shoe caught the lacquered
rawhide of the other

and pitched me
into the unforgiving

crotch of a yellow birch.
From a breathless heap

of middleage parts, I
looked up through torn

banners of bark
to see the guardian

angel of my regrets
coming at me with the sunlight

cutting through fog, dropping in
to guarantee I'd never

forget what kind
of slime would scheme

to leave his wife
and infant boy while pretending

everything was strawberries
and cream to a father

now an angel with a temporary
license to see right

through the thin skin of my
cock and bull to the self-

centered chicken shit. He drove
his chest hard into mine

and started to count.
I tried not to blink,

memorizing the charred
smear of his frown edged

with glee, but just
as I began to speculate

whether all supernatural beings
had to keep track of each

second they embraced
the living, and before

I could think to apologize
or take a breath, he slapped

the white mat and faded
into a pale ribbon tracing

the melt-fed mountain
brook that drives winter

out of the smallmouth
bass-and-beaver sanctuary

where, when the killdeer
shrieks and flaps its outspread

wings against the bank,
I wade into the still

center of summer
and bait my hook.

Roger Weingarten

is the author of eight volumes of poetry and co-editor of three
anthologies, including *New American Poets of the '90s* (Godine,
1991). His poems and essays have appeared in magazines including
*The American Poetry Review, Poetry, The New Yorker, The Paris
Review, Ploughshares, The New Republic,* and other magazines. He
has been a fellow of the Ingram Merrill Foundation, the Dana
Foundation, and the National Endowment for the Arts. He teaches
in, and directs, the MFA in Writing Program at Vermont College.